God's Plan for Plants

by
Judy Hull Moore

Edited by Delores Shimmin

Library of Congress Cataloging in Publication Data

Moore, Judy Hull.
  God's plan for plants.

  SUMMARY: Describes the usefulness of plants that God has
given us.
  1. Plants—Juvenile literature. 2. Plants, Useful—Juvenile
literature. 3. Nature—Religious interpretations—Juvenile literature.
[1. Plants]   I. Shimmin, Delores.   II. Title.
QK49.M83   581   80-17800
ISBN 0-8024-3065-1

MOODY PRESS ● CHICAGO

©1976, by
A Beka Book Publications
Moody Press Edition, 1980

BN: 0-8024-3065-1

Plants are a very important part
of God's plan.

We need plants to live.

Without plants,
there could be
no life at all.

Animals use plants to make homes.

We use plants to make our homes, too.

We need plants to live.
We need milk to
    grow strong.
The cow eats
    grass.

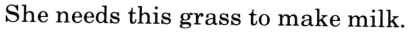

She needs this grass to make milk.
Most food that God gives us
    comes from plants.
    Without plants,
    we would not be
    very strong.

When we get sick, we need medicine
to help us get well.
Some medicines are made from plants.

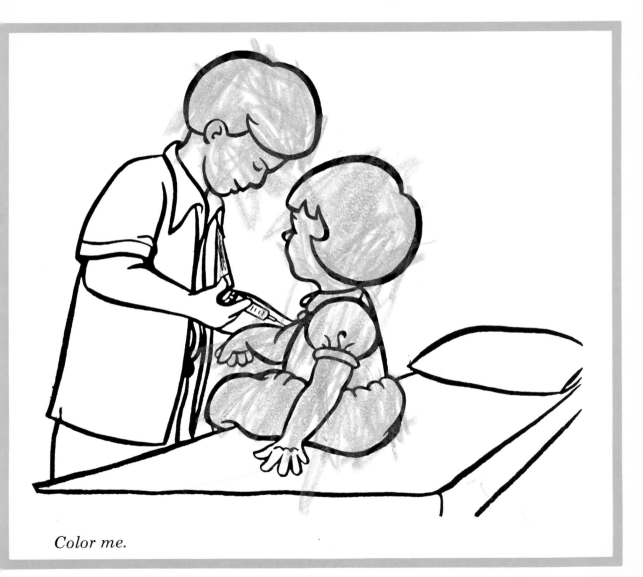

Color me.

Meg has a new cotton
dress.
Cotton comes from
a plant.

Color the cotton.

We eat some stems of plants.

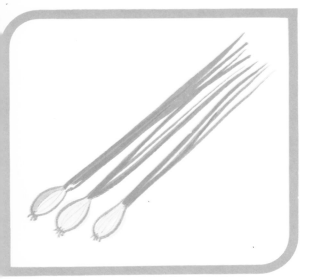

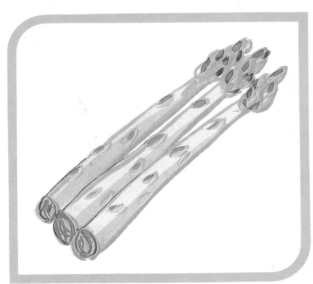

It is the leaves' job to make food
for the plant.
Leaves also make food for us.
It takes the work of about
thirty leaves to make one
big, round apple.

We eat some leaves of plants.

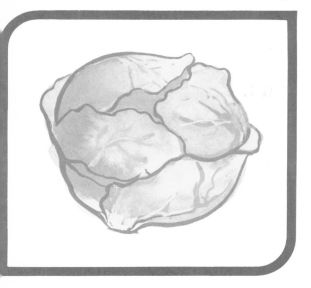

It is the flower's job to make
seeds for new plants.
Some flowers are colorful
and smell very sweet.
Some flowers are not colorful
and do not have any smell.

We eat fruit that comes from flowers.
We also eat seeds that flowers make.

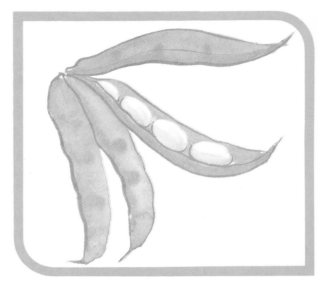

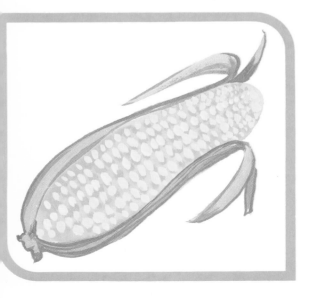

Color me in the tree.

18

뉴욕한인
교회장서

There are hundreds of thousands of kinds
of plants.
Some are so tiny you cannot see them.
Some are huge.
A tree trunk is the
    largest stem in
    the plant world.

Thank you, God, for plants.